REAL ESTATE INVESTING

A Short, Powerful, and Easy-to-Follow Guide for Navigating Your First Deal and Beyond

SUMMER YESIL

CONTENTS

Chapter I   02
Why Invest in Real Estate? + the Basics

Chapter II   06
Setting Your Investment Goals and Strategy

Chapter III   11
Building Your Real Estate Knowledge Base

Chapter IV   14
Financing Your First Deal

Chapter V   21
Finding and Evaluating Properties

Chapter VI   26
Conducting Due Diligence

Chapter VII   32
Making an Offer and Negotiating the Deal

Chapter VIII   37
Managing Your Investment Property

Chapter IX   43
Scaling Your Real Estate Portfolio

Chapter X   48
Navigating Market Changes and Future Trends

Preface

Welcome to the world of real estate investing! If you're anything like I was when I started, you're probably feeling a mix of excitement and "what the heck have I gotten myself into?" Don't worry, that's totally normal. I'm here to guide you through it, and by the end of this book, you will gain so much insight into how to use real estate to your financial advantage.

Real estate investing has completely transformed my life—allowing me to break free from the daily grind of a 9-to-5 job, achieve financial independence, and build generational wealth. Now, I enjoy consistent income that flows in whether I'm working or not, and let me tell you, there's nothing quite like the freedom and perks that comes with that. But here's the thing: becoming financially literate was the first stepping stone to all of this. Understanding how money works, especially in real estate, is your gateway to true wealth. So, let's dive in together and get you started on this incredible journey!

Chapter 1: Why Invest in Real Estate? + the Basics

Why Invest in Real Estate?

Let's get into why real estate is, in my humble opinion, one of the best ways to build wealth. First off, real estate gives you multiple ways to make money. You've got rental income, property appreciation (fancy talk for the value going up), and profits from selling at the right time. It's like having multiple streams of income from one investment—pretty sweet, right?

Another reason I love real estate is that it's a great hedge against inflation. As prices go up, so do rents and property values. So, while everything else gets more expensive, your real estate investments are busy keeping pace. It's like having a built-in financial bodyguard.

And let's not forget the tax advantages. The government loves real estate investors (well, sort of). You can deduct mortgage interest, property taxes, and a bunch of other expenses. Plus, depreciation is like this magical, non-cash deduction that lowers your taxable income. It's like finding money in your pocket that you didn't know you had.

Finally, real estate gives you control. Unlike stocks, where you're at the mercy of the market, with real estate, you're the boss. You get to make decisions that directly affect your bottom line, whether it's choosing tenants, setting rent, or deciding which trendy backsplash to install in the kitchen.

Overview of Real Estate Investing

Let's start with the basics. Real estate investing is essentially the art of making money from properties. We're talking about buying, owning, managing, renting, and eventually selling real estate to turn a profit. Unlike stocks or that vintage handbag collection you've been curating, real estate is a tangible asset—you can actually walk up to it, touch it, and maybe even renovate it with some Pinterest-inspired flair.

Now, there are different flavors of real estate investments, kind of like ice cream but without the calories:

1. **Residential Properties**: This is where most of us dip our toes in the water. Think single-family

homes, cute little duplexes, or even that trendy downtown condo. Residential properties are great because they're familiar, and you can generate rental income to cover your expenses—and hopefully sip a margarita on the beach with what's left over.

2. **Commercial Properties**: If residential is the gateway, commercial is where you go when you're ready to level up. This includes office buildings, retail spaces, and warehouses. It's more complex and often pricier, but the rewards can be worth it.

3. **Real Estate Investment Trusts (REITs)**: Not ready to buy a building yet? No problem! REITs let you invest in real estate through the stock market. It's like being a property owner without the headaches of dealing with tenants or leaky roofs. You just sit back, relax, and collect dividends.

4. **Land:** Raw land is a bit like a blank canvas—it can be anything you want, but it requires vision and patience. If you pick the right spot, you might just strike gold when development rolls into town.

Key Concepts and Terminology

Before we dive headfirst into the deep end, let's cover a few key terms:

- **Cash Flow:** This is the money left over after you've paid all your property expenses. Positive cash flow means you're making money—kind of the point, right?
- **Appreciation:** When your property's value goes up over time, it's like your investment aging like fine wine. Cheers to that!
- **Equity:** The difference between what your property is worth and what you owe on it.
- **Cap Rate (Capitalization Rate):** This is a fancy way of saying, "What's my return on investment?" It's a quick way to compare how different properties stack up.

With these basics under your belt, you're ready to start exploring the wonderful world of real estate investing. Trust me, it's a wild ride, but with a little knowledge and a lot of determination, you'll be well on your way to navigating your first deal like a pro. Now, let's get to work!

Chapter 2: Setting Your Investment Goals and Strategy

Alright, now that you've dipped your toes into the world of real estate investing, it's time to get serious about your goals and strategy. Setting clear, actionable goals is the foundation of any successful investment journey. Without a roadmap, it's easy to get lost or distracted. So, let's talk about how to define your goals and choose the right strategy that aligns with where you want to go.

Defining Your Why

Before we dive into the nitty-gritty of goals and strategy, let's take a moment to reflect on your "why." Why do you want to invest in real estate? Is it to achieve financial freedom, generate a steady stream of income, or maybe leave a legacy for your family? Understanding your motivation will help you stay focused and committed, even when challenges arise.

For me, my "why" was clear from the beginning: I wanted to break free from the limitations of a traditional 9-to-5 job, create a life where I had control over my time, and build a financial cushion that could support me and my loved ones for years to come. Knowing this kept me motivated through the ups and downs of my investment journey, and it will do the same for you.

Take some time to reflect on what drives you. Write it down. This will be your anchor, especially on days when the real estate market feels more like a roller coaster than a smooth ride.

Setting SMART Goals

Once you've defined your "why," it's time to translate that into specific, actionable goals. This is where the concept of SMART goals comes into play. SMART stands for Specific, Measurable, Achievable, Relevant, and Time-bound. Let's break that down:

- **Specific:** Your goals should be clear and precise. Instead of saying, "I want to make money in real estate," say, "I want to acquire my first rental property within the next six months."
- **Measurable:** You need a way to track your progress. If your goal is to generate $1,000 per month in passive income, you can measure how close you are to achieving that by looking at your rental income statements.

- **Achievable:** While it's great to dream big, your goals should also be realistic. If you're just starting out, aiming to acquire ten properties in your first year might be setting yourself up for disappointment. Start with one, then build from there.
- **Relevant:** Your goals should align with your overall "why." If your main motivation is to achieve financial independence, focus on investments that generate steady cash flow rather than speculative deals.
- **Time-bound:** Every goal needs a deadline. This creates a sense of urgency and helps you stay on track. For example, "I will save $20,000 for a down payment by the end of this year."

By setting SMART goals, you're not just daydreaming—you're creating a concrete plan that will guide your decisions and actions.

Choosing the Right Investment Strategy

Now that you've set your goals, it's time to choose a strategy that will help you achieve them. There are several real estate investment strategies, each with its own advantages and risks. The key is to find the one that aligns with your goals, risk tolerance, and available resources.

1. **Buy and Hold**: This strategy involves purchasing a property and holding onto it for the long term, while renting it out to generate income. It's a popular choice for those seeking steady cash flow and long-term appreciation.

2. **Fix and Flip**: If you enjoy rolling up your sleeves and taking on projects, fixing and flipping might be for you. This strategy involves buying properties that need some TLC, renovating them, and selling them for a profit. It's riskier but can be highly rewarding if done right.

3. **House Hacking**: A great option for beginners, house hacking involves buying a multi-family property, living in one unit, and renting out the others. This allows you to generate rental income while keeping your living expenses low.

4. **Wholesaling**: Wholesaling is a strategy where you find a property at a great price, put it under contract, and then sell that contract to another investor for a fee. It requires minimal capital but demands a good understanding of the market and strong negotiation skills.

5. **REITs (Real Estate Investment Trusts)**: If you're looking for a more hands-off approach, investing in REITs allows you to own shares in a portfolio of real estate assets. It's like investing in real estate without having to deal with tenants or maintenance.

Each of these strategies has its pros and cons, and the best one for you will depend on your specific goals, financial situation, and how involved you want to be in the process. As you explore these options, remember that your strategy can evolve over time as you gain experience and confidence.

Setting your investment goals and choosing the right strategy are crucial steps in your real estate journey. With clear goals and a solid plan, you'll be well on your way to achieving the financial freedom and independence that real estate investing can offer.

Chapter 3: Building Your Real Estate Knowledge Base

Now that you've set your goals and chosen a strategy, it's time to dive into the education phase of your real estate journey. Knowledge is your most valuable asset as an investor, and the more you know, the better equipped you'll be to make informed decisions and navigate the challenges ahead. In this chapter, we'll explore how to build a solid real estate knowledge base, understand market dynamics, and the importance of networking within the industry.

Learning Resources: Where to Start

When I first got into real estate, I was overwhelmed by how much there was to learn. But here's the good news: there's a wealth of resources out there, and many of them are free or inexpensive. The key is to start with the basics and gradually build your knowledge.

Books: There are countless real estate investing books that cater to beginners. Some classics that I always recommend include *"Rich Dad Poor Dad"* by Robert Kiyosaki, which introduces the mindset needed for financial success, and *"The Millionaire Real Estate Investor"* by Gary Keller, which provides a practical guide to building wealth through real estate.

Podcasts: If you're like me and love to multitask, podcasts are a fantastic way to absorb information on the go. Shows like *"BiggerPockets Real Estate Podcast"* and *"The Real Estate Guys Radio Show"* offer insights from experienced investors and cover a wide range of topics, from financing to property management.

Online Courses: There are numerous online platforms offering courses on real estate investing. Websites like Udemy, Coursera, and even YouTube can provide valuable lessons on everything from analyzing deals to understanding tax benefits.

Blogs and Forums: The internet is brimming with real estate blogs and forums where investors share their experiences and advice. Websites like BiggerPockets have active communities where you can ask questions, share your progress, and learn from others who've been where you are.

Start with one or two of these resources and gradually expand your learning. It's important not to get overwhelmed by trying to consume too much information at once. Focus on what's relevant to your current stage in the investment process.

Understanding the Market: Location, Location, Location

One of the most critical aspects of real estate investing is understanding the market you're investing in. This is where the famous phrase "location, location, location" comes into play. The location of a property can significantly impact its value, rental income potential, and appreciation.

To effectively analyze a market, you need to look at several factors:

1. **Economic Indicators:** Pay attention to the local economy, including job growth, unemployment rates, and major industries. A strong local economy usually leads to a healthy real estate market, as people move to areas with abundant job opportunities.
2. **Population Growth:** Areas with increasing population numbers tend to have higher demand for

housing, which can drive up property values and rents. Look for cities or neighborhoods with a growing population.

3. **Supply and Demand:** Research the balance between the number of available properties and the demand for housing. If there's a shortage of available homes, prices are likely to rise. Conversely, if there's an oversupply, it might be harder to find tenants or sell a property.

4. **Neighborhood Dynamics:** Delve into the specifics of the neighborhood. Are there good schools, amenities, and transportation links? Is the area considered safe? These factors will influence both the desirability of the property and its long-term appreciation.

5. **Market Trends:** Study the historical data and trends in the market. Are property values and rental prices rising, stable, or declining? Understanding these trends will help you make informed decisions about where and when to invest.

Networking: The Power of Connections

Real estate is as much about people as it is about properties. Building a strong network can open doors to opportunities, provide support, and offer valuable insights that you won't find in books or online courses.

Start by attending local real estate meetups, joining investor groups, or participating in online forums. Networking with other investors, real estate agents, lenders, and contractors can help you build relationships that will be invaluable as you grow your investment portfolio.

Additionally, finding a mentor—someone who has been successful in the type of real estate investing you're interested in—can be a game-changer. A mentor can offer guidance, answer your questions, and help you avoid common pitfalls.

In the end, building your real estate knowledge base is about continuous learning and staying curious. The more you know, the more confident you'll be in making smart investment decisions. Real estate markets change, new opportunities arise, and challenges will inevitably come your way. By committing to lifelong learning and surrounding yourself with the right people, you'll be well-prepared to navigate the world of real estate investing with success.

Chapter 4: Financing Your First Deal

So, you've got your goals set and your knowledge base is growing—fantastic! Now it's time to tackle one of the most crucial aspects of real estate investing: financing your first deal. Understanding your financing options and how to secure funds is essential to making your investment dreams a reality. Let's break it down step by step.

Understanding Financing Options

When it comes to financing a real estate investment, there are several avenues you can explore. Each option has its own set of advantages and requirements, so it's important to choose the one that aligns with your financial situation and investment goals.

1. **Traditional Mortgages**: This is the most common method for financing real estate. With a traditional mortgage, you'll work with a lender to borrow money to purchase the property. The loan is typically repaid over 15 to 30 years with a fixed or adjustable interest rate. To qualify, you'll need a good credit score, a stable income, and a down payment (usually 20% of the purchase price). If

you're new to investing, this is often the go-to option.

2. **FHA Loans**: If you're a first-time homebuyer or have less-than-perfect credit, an FHA (Federal Housing Administration) loan might be a viable option. FHA loans are backed by the government and typically require a lower down payment—sometimes as little as 3.5%. However, you'll need to meet certain income and credit requirements, and the property must meet specific standards.

3. **VA Loans**: For veterans and active-duty service members, VA (Veterans Affairs) loans offer a great opportunity. These loans are backed by the VA and often require no down payment. They also come with favorable terms, such as lower interest rates and no private mortgage insurance (PMI). However, they are only available for properties that will be used as a primary residence.

4. **Hard Money Loans**: If you're looking to finance a property quickly or need funds for a short-term project (like a fix-and-flip), hard money loans can be a good option. These loans are typically provided by private lenders and are based more on the value of the property than your creditworthiness. They come with higher interest rates and shorter

repayment terms, so they're best suited for quick, high-return investments.

5.   **Seller Financing**: In some cases, the property seller may be willing to finance part or all of the purchase price. This means you make payments directly to the seller rather than a bank. Seller financing can be beneficial if you're having trouble securing traditional financing, but it requires good negotiation skills and a solid relationship with the seller.

6.   **Partnerships**: If you don't have all the capital you need, consider partnering with someone who does. This could be a friend, family member, or fellow investor. Partnerships can provide the necessary funds and also offer opportunities for shared expertise and resources.

How to Qualify for a Mortgage

Qualifying for a mortgage or loan requires more than just filling out an application. Lenders will assess your financial situation to ensure you're a reliable borrower. Here are some key factors they'll consider:

1.   **Credit Score**: Your credit score is a critical factor in determining your eligibility for a mortgage

and the interest rate you'll receive. Aim for a score of 700 or higher for the best rates. If your score needs improvement, take steps to pay down debt and address any inaccuracies on your credit report.

2. **Income:** Lenders want to see that you have a stable income to cover your mortgage payments. Be prepared to provide proof of income, such as pay stubs, tax returns, or bank statements. Self-employed individuals might need to show additional documentation.

3. **Down Payment:** The amount you can put down upfront will impact your loan options. Traditional loans typically require 20%, but some programs, like FHA loans, may accept less. Saving for a down payment can be one of the biggest hurdles, so start early and consider ways to increase your savings.

4. **Debt-to-Income Ratio:** This ratio compares your monthly debt payments to your gross monthly income. Lenders use it to assess your ability to manage additional debt. Generally, a ratio of 43% or lower is preferred, though some lenders may accept slightly higher ratios.

Creative Financing for Beginners

If you're new to investing and traditional financing options seem out of reach, there are creative ways to secure funding:

- **Crowdfunding**: Real estate crowdfunding platforms allow you to pool money from multiple investors to fund a project. This can be a way to get involved with real estate with less capital upfront.
- **Home Equity Loans**: If you own a home with significant equity, you might consider a home equity loan or line of credit (HELOC) to fund your real estate investment.
- **Retirement Accounts**: Some investors use funds from retirement accounts, like a self-directed IRA, to invest in real estate. Be sure to consult with a financial advisor to understand the implications and regulations.

Securing financing for your first real estate deal can seem daunting, but with a clear understanding of your options and requirements, you'll be better equipped to make the best choice for your investment. Remember, whether you're using traditional methods or exploring creative avenues, thorough research and preparation are key to successful real estate investing.

Chapter 5: Finding and Evaluating Properties

Congratulations on making it this far! With your goals set, knowledge gained, and financing options lined up, it's time to dive into one of the most exciting parts of real estate investing: finding and evaluating properties. This is where the rubber meets the road, and your ability to identify promising investments will make all the difference. Let's explore how to find the right property and assess its potential to ensure you make smart investment choices.

Finding the Right Property

Finding a great property requires a blend of research, patience, and a bit of intuition. Here are some strategies to help you locate potential investment opportunities:

1. **Online Property Listings**: Websites like Zillow, Realtor.com, and Redfin are valuable resources for browsing available properties. Set up alerts for properties that meet your criteria to stay updated on new listings. Pay attention to the "Days

on Market" statistic, as it can give you insight into how long properties are sitting unsold.

2. **Real Estate Agents**: Working with a knowledgeable real estate agent can be incredibly beneficial, especially if you're new to the market. Agents often have access to off-market deals and can help you navigate the buying process. Look for agents who specialize in investment properties and have experience with the type of property you're interested in.

3. **Networking**: Let your network know you're in the market for investment properties. Sometimes the best deals come from word-of-mouth referrals. Attend local real estate meetups, join investment groups, and connect with other investors to uncover potential opportunities.

4. **Direct Mail Campaigns**: Sending targeted mail to property owners in specific areas can yield results. For example, you might send postcards to owners of vacant properties or distressed homes. This proactive approach can help you find motivated sellers who are looking to offload their properties quickly.

5. **Driving for Dollars**: This old-school method involves driving through neighborhoods and looking for signs of distressed properties—overgrown lawns,

boarded-up windows, or "For Sale by Owner" signs. It's a hands-on approach that can lead to finding properties that haven't yet hit the market.

Evaluating Property Potential

Once you've identified a potential property, it's crucial to evaluate its investment potential. This involves a detailed analysis of various factors to determine whether the property will meet your financial goals. Here's how to evaluate a property effectively:

1. **Location Analysis:** As the saying goes, location is everything. Research the neighborhood to ensure it aligns with your investment strategy. Look for factors such as proximity to schools, public transportation, and amenities. Check crime rates and consider the overall desirability of the area. A great location can significantly impact rental income and property appreciation.
2. **Property Condition:** Assess the physical condition of the property. If it's a fixer-upper, estimate the cost of repairs and renovations. Look for signs of structural issues, such as foundation cracks or water damage. The condition of major systems—like the roof, HVAC, and plumbing—should

also be evaluated. A home inspection can provide a detailed report on the property's condition and uncover hidden issues.

3. **Comparable Sales (Comps)**: Analyze recent sales of similar properties in the area to gauge the property's value. Comps provide insight into what buyers are willing to pay and can help you determine a fair purchase price. Your real estate agent can assist with this analysis, or you can use online tools to find recent sales data.

4. **Cash Flow Analysis**: For rental properties, calculate the potential cash flow by comparing rental income to expenses. Include mortgage payments, property taxes, insurance, maintenance, and property management fees. A positive cash flow indicates that the property will generate more income than it costs to operate, which is essential for long-term success.

5. **Cap Rate Calculation**: The capitalization rate, or cap rate, is a measure of the property's return on investment. It's calculated by dividing the property's net operating income (NOI) by its purchase price. A higher cap rate generally indicates a better return on investment, but it's important to balance cap rate with other factors, such as property condition and location.

6. **Future Appreciation:** Consider the potential for future property value appreciation. Research local development plans, upcoming infrastructure projects, and economic growth in the area. Properties in rapidly growing or revitalizing areas often experience higher appreciation rates.

Making the Decision

After evaluating the property, weigh all factors to make an informed decision. Consider how the property aligns with your investment goals, whether it fits your budget, and if it offers the potential for the returns you're seeking. Don't rush the decision—take your time to ensure you're making a smart investment.

Finding and evaluating properties can be both thrilling and challenging, but with a clear strategy and thorough analysis, you'll be well-prepared to identify opportunities that align with your investment goals. Remember, the success of your real estate investment journey hinges on your ability to choose the right properties and make informed decisions. Happy hunting!

Chapter 6: Conducting Due Diligence

Congratulations, you've found a property that looks promising and meets your investment criteria! But before you sign on the dotted line and make an offer, there's one crucial step you can't afford to skip: conducting due diligence. This phase is all about thoroughly vetting the property to ensure it's a sound investment. Skipping due diligence can lead to costly mistakes and unforeseen issues, so let's dive into the key aspects of this process to help you make an informed decision.

What is Due Diligence?

Due diligence is the process of investigating a property to uncover any potential issues or risks that could impact your investment. It involves a comprehensive review of various factors, including the property's condition, legal status, financial performance, and market environment. The goal is to confirm that the property aligns with your investment goals and that you're aware of any potential red flags.

Property Inspection

One of the most critical components of due diligence is the property inspection. A thorough inspection can reveal hidden issues that might not be apparent during a casual walk-through. Here's what to focus on:

1. **Structural Integrity**: Check for any signs of structural problems, such as foundation cracks, sagging floors, or roof damage. Structural issues can be costly to repair and may affect the property's long-term value.

2. **Systems and Appliances**: Inspect major systems like HVAC, plumbing, and electrical. Make sure appliances are in working order and look for signs of wear or potential failure. Addressing these issues before purchase can save you from unexpected expenses down the road.

3. **Pest and Mold Issues**: Look for signs of pest infestations or mold. These problems can cause significant damage and may require expensive remediation. A professional pest and mold inspection can provide a detailed assessment.

4. **Safety and Code Compliance**: Ensure the property meets local building codes and safety standards. Check for issues such as inadequate

smoke detectors, unsafe staircases, or non-compliant electrical wiring. Safety should always be a priority.

Reviewing Property Documents

Next, review all relevant property documents to verify its legal and financial standing. This includes:

1. **Title Report:** Obtain a title report to confirm that the property has a clear title and is free of any liens or encumbrances. This report will show the current ownership and any legal claims against the property.
2. **Property Disclosures:** Review the seller's property disclosure statement, which should detail any known issues or defects with the property. While this document can provide valuable information, it's important to verify the details through your inspection.
3. **Lease Agreements:** If the property is already rented, review existing lease agreements. Check the terms of the leases, rental income, and tenant history. This will help you understand the property's cash flow and any obligations you'll inherit as the new owner.
4. **HOA Documents:** If the property is part of a homeowners association (HOA), review the HOA's

rules, regulations, and financial statements. Understand any fees or restrictions associated with the property and how they may impact your investment.

Financial Analysis

Conduct a thorough financial analysis to ensure the property meets your investment criteria:

1. **Current Financial Performance**: Analyze the property's current income and expenses. Compare rental income to operating costs, including property management fees, maintenance, and taxes. Make sure the property generates positive cash flow or fits within your financial goals.
2. **Future Financial Projections**: Estimate future expenses and income to gauge the property's long-term viability. Consider factors such as potential rent increases, property tax changes, and maintenance costs.
3. **Investment Metrics**: Review key investment metrics such as cap rate, cash-on-cash return, and return on investment (ROI). Ensure these metrics align with your investment strategy and expectations.

Market Analysis

Finally, conduct a market analysis to understand the property's potential for appreciation and rental demand:

1. **Comparable Sales (Comps):** Revisit the comps you reviewed earlier and see if there have been any recent changes in the market. This will help you validate the property's value and understand current market trends.
2. **Market Trends:** Research local market trends, including supply and demand, economic indicators, and upcoming developments. Understanding these trends will help you gauge the property's potential for future growth.
3. **Neighborhood Assessment:** Reassess the neighborhood to confirm its desirability and growth potential. Look for new amenities, infrastructure projects, or other factors that could impact the property's value.

Final Decision

After completing your due diligence, review all the information you've gathered and make an informed decision. If the property checks all your boxes and aligns with your investment goals, you can proceed with confidence. If any red flags or issues arise, weigh the risks and consider whether they are manageable or if you should continue your search.

Conducting thorough due diligence is essential for protecting your investment and ensuring a successful real estate venture. By meticulously evaluating the property, reviewing documents, analyzing finances, and understanding the market, you'll be well-equipped to make a sound investment decision.

Chapter 7: Making an Offer and Negotiating the Deal

You've found the perfect property, completed your due diligence, and you're ready to take the next big step: making an offer and negotiating the deal. This part of the process is where your strategic thinking and negotiation skills come into play. A well-crafted offer and effective negotiation can secure the best terms for your investment and set the stage for a successful transaction. Let's break down how to approach making an offer and negotiating effectively.

Crafting Your Offer

Making an offer involves more than just stating a price—it's about presenting a compelling case that aligns with both your investment goals and the seller's expectations. Here's how to craft an offer that stands out:

1. **Determine Your Offer Price:** Based on your market analysis and due diligence, determine a fair offer price for the property. Consider factors such as comparable sales, property condition, and your

financial goals. Aim for a price that reflects the property's value but also leaves room for negotiation.

2. **Include Contingencies**: Contingencies are conditions that must be met for the sale to proceed. Common contingencies include financing, appraisal, and inspection. Including these in your offer protects you by allowing you to back out or renegotiate if issues arise. Be sure to clearly outline these contingencies in your offer to avoid any misunderstandings.

3. **Offer Earnest Money**: Earnest money is a deposit made to demonstrate your seriousness about the purchase. It's typically a small percentage of the offer price, and it will be applied to the purchase price if the deal goes through. Offering a reasonable amount of earnest money can strengthen your offer and show the seller that you're committed.

4. **Draft a Strong Offer Letter**: A personalized offer letter can sometimes sway the seller's decision. Include details about why you're interested in the property, your investment goals, and any personal touches that might resonate with the seller. This letter can set you apart from other buyers and create a positive impression.

Negotiating the Deal

Once you've submitted your offer, be prepared for negotiations. This is where your skills and strategy come into play:

1. **Be Prepared for Counteroffers:** Sellers may respond with a counteroffer, which could involve changes to the price, contingencies, or other terms. Be prepared to review and respond to these counteroffers thoughtfully. Consider whether the changes are acceptable or if you need to negotiate further.

2. **Negotiate Terms Beyond Price:** While the offer price is important, other terms can also be negotiable. Consider discussing items such as the closing date, repairs or improvements, and who will cover closing costs. Flexibility on these terms can sometimes lead to a better overall deal.

3. **Leverage Market Conditions:** Use your understanding of the current market conditions to your advantage. If it's a buyer's market with many available properties, you might have more negotiating power. Conversely, in a seller's market with high demand, you may need to be more flexible with your terms.

4. **Maintain Professionalism and Patience:** Negotiations can be a delicate process. Maintain a

professional demeanor and be patient. Avoid making emotional decisions and focus on achieving a deal that aligns with your investment goals. Building a good rapport with the seller and their agent can also be beneficial.

5. **Know When to Walk Away**: Not every negotiation will lead to a successful deal. Be prepared to walk away if the terms don't meet your criteria or if the property no longer aligns with your investment goals. Sometimes, the best decision is to move on and find another opportunity.

Finalizing the Agreement

Once you and the seller agree on the terms, it's time to finalize the agreement:

1. **Review the Purchase Agreement**: Carefully review the purchase agreement, ensuring that all agreed-upon terms are included and accurately reflected. Consider having a real estate attorney review the document to ensure there are no legal issues or unfavorable terms.

2. **Complete Required Documentation**: Provide any necessary documentation, such as proof of financing and identification, to proceed with the

purchase. Ensure that all paperwork is completed accurately and submitted on time.

3. **Schedule a Final Walk-Through**: Before closing, schedule a final walk-through of the property to ensure it's in the condition agreed upon and that any required repairs or changes have been made. This final inspection helps confirm that the property meets your expectations before you finalize the purchase.

Closing the Deal

With the offer accepted and negotiations complete, you're almost there! The final step is to close the deal, which involves signing the closing documents, transferring funds, and officially taking ownership of the property. Work closely with your real estate agent, attorney, and lender to ensure a smooth closing process.

Making an offer and negotiating the deal are pivotal moments in your real estate investment journey. By crafting a well-considered offer, negotiating effectively, and finalizing the agreement with care, you'll be well on your way to securing a successful investment. Remember, a thoughtful and strategic approach can make all the difference in achieving your investment goals.

Chapter 8: Managing Your Investment Property

You've made a savvy investment and closed the deal—kudos! Now, it's time to roll up your sleeves and dive into property management. This phase is crucial for maintaining the value of your investment and ensuring a steady income stream. Whether you're managing the property yourself or working with a property management company, understanding the ins and outs of property management will help you keep everything running smoothly. Let's break down the essentials of managing your investment property.

Tenant Management

One of the most important aspects of property management is handling tenant relations. Your goal is to attract reliable tenants who will take good care of the property and pay rent on time. Here's how to manage tenant relationships effectively:

1. **Screening and Selection:** Begin by implementing a thorough tenant screening process. This includes checking credit scores, rental histories, and employment status. A comprehensive application process helps ensure that you select tenants who are financially stable and responsible. Consider including a background check and verification of references to gain a full picture of potential renters.

2. **Lease Agreements:** Draft a clear and detailed lease agreement outlining all terms and conditions, including rent amount, payment due dates, security deposits, and responsibilities for maintenance and repairs. A well-crafted lease agreement protects both you and the tenant and sets expectations for the duration of the rental.

3. **Rent Collection:** Establish a streamlined rent collection process. Offer multiple payment options, such as online payments or checks, to accommodate tenants' preferences. Implement a system for tracking payments and managing late fees. Consistent rent collection is vital for maintaining cash flow and ensuring that your investment remains profitable.

4. **Communication and Responsiveness:** Foster open and professional communication with your

tenants. Address any concerns or maintenance requests promptly to maintain tenant satisfaction and minimize issues. A responsive and approachable attitude can help build a positive landlord-tenant relationship and reduce turnover.

Property Maintenance

Regular maintenance and prompt repairs are key to preserving the value of your property and keeping tenants happy:

1.   **Routine Maintenance:** Create a maintenance schedule for regular tasks, such as lawn care, gutter cleaning, and HVAC servicing. Routine maintenance helps prevent small issues from becoming major problems and ensures that the property remains in good condition.

2.   **Repairs and Emergencies:** Respond quickly to repair requests and address any issues that arise. Establish a network of reliable contractors and service providers to handle repairs and emergencies efficiently. Keeping the property in good repair enhances tenant satisfaction and can help prevent costly damage.

3.   **Property Inspections:** Conduct periodic property inspections to assess the condition of the

property and identify any maintenance needs. Schedule inspections before and after tenant move-ins and periodically during the lease term. Inspections help you stay on top of any issues and ensure that the property is being well maintained.

Financial Management

Effective financial management is crucial for maximizing the profitability of your investment property:

1.   **Budgeting and Expense Tracking**: Develop a budget that outlines all property-related expenses, including mortgage payments, property taxes, insurance, maintenance, and management fees. Track expenses meticulously to ensure you stay within budget and plan for unexpected costs. Regularly review your budget to make adjustments as needed.

2.   **Record-Keeping**: Maintain accurate records of all financial transactions related to the property. This includes rent payments, repairs, utility bills, and other expenses. Detailed record-keeping simplifies tax preparation and provides a clear picture of the property's financial performance.

3. **Tax Considerations**: Familiarize yourself with the tax implications of owning and managing rental property. Understand deductible expenses, such as property management fees, repairs, and depreciation. Consulting with a tax professional can help you navigate tax regulations and maximize deductions.

Professional vs. Self-Management

Deciding whether to manage the property yourself or hire a professional property management company depends on your preferences, time availability, and investment goals:

- **Self-Management**: Managing the property yourself can save on management fees and give you direct control over all aspects of property management. However, it requires time, effort, and knowledge of property management responsibilities.
- **Professional Management**: A property management company can handle day-to-day tasks, including tenant screening, rent collection, maintenance, and legal compliance. While this option involves management fees, it can be a good choice if you prefer a hands-off approach or own multiple properties.

Legal and Regulatory Compliance

Ensure you comply with all local, state, and federal regulations related to rental properties. This includes understanding landlord-tenant laws, fair housing regulations, and building codes. Staying informed and compliant helps avoid legal issues and maintain a positive reputation as a landlord.

Managing an investment property requires attention to detail, strong organizational skills, and a proactive approach. By focusing on tenant management, property maintenance, financial management, and legal compliance, you'll set the stage for a successful and profitable real estate investment. Effective property management is the key to maximizing your investment's potential and achieving long-term success in the real estate market.

Chapter 9: Scaling Your Real Estate Portfolio

You've successfully navigated the initial stages of real estate investing, from finding your first property to managing it effectively. Now, you might be considering expanding your real estate portfolio. Scaling up can significantly increase your income and grow your wealth, but it also comes with its own set of challenges and considerations. In this chapter, we'll explore how to strategically expand your real estate investments and manage a larger portfolio successfully.

Understanding the Benefits of Scaling

Expanding your real estate portfolio can offer several advantages:

1. **Increased Cash Flow**: More properties typically mean more rental income. By carefully selecting and managing additional properties, you can significantly boost your monthly cash flow and overall financial stability.
2. **Diversification**: A larger portfolio allows for diversification, reducing the risk associated with relying on a single property or market. Diversifying

across different types of properties or geographic locations can protect your investments from market fluctuations.

3. **Economies of Scale**: As you acquire more properties, you can benefit from economies of scale. This might include negotiating better terms with contractors, property managers, or lenders due to the increased volume of work or business you bring.

4. **Wealth Building**: A larger portfolio contributes to building generational wealth. Real estate can appreciate over time, and owning multiple properties enhances your ability to accumulate assets and grow your net worth.

Strategic Planning for Expansion

Before scaling your portfolio, it's essential to have a clear plan. Here's how to approach the process:

1. **Assess Your Current Situation**: Evaluate your existing properties to understand their performance and how they fit into your investment strategy. Review your financial position, including your cash flow, equity, and financing options. This assessment will help you determine how many additional properties you can realistically manage and afford.

2. **Set Clear Goals**: Define your expansion goals. Are you looking to increase cash flow, diversify your investments, or build long-term wealth? Having clear objectives will guide your investment strategy and help you stay focused.

3. **Expand Your Network**: Building a larger portfolio often requires working with a broader network of real estate professionals. Strengthen relationships with real estate agents, property managers, contractors, and lenders. A strong network can provide valuable insights and opportunities for acquiring new properties.

4. **Explore Financing Options**: Determine how you'll finance additional properties. Options may include traditional mortgages, private loans, or leveraging the equity in your existing properties. Evaluate different financing methods to find the best fit for your investment strategy.

Finding and Evaluating New Properties

When adding properties to your portfolio, maintaining a disciplined approach is crucial:

1. **Market Research**: Conduct thorough market research to identify promising locations for investment. Look for areas with strong rental

demand, potential for appreciation, and favorable economic conditions. Stay updated on market trends and local developments that could impact property values.

2. **Due Diligence:** Apply the same rigorous due diligence process to new properties as you did with your first investment. Evaluate the property's condition, financial performance, and potential risks. Conduct inspections, review financial documents, and analyze the local market to ensure each property aligns with your investment goals.

3. **Property Management:** As your portfolio grows, managing multiple properties can become more complex. Consider hiring a professional property management company if you haven't already. They can handle day-to-day operations, tenant relations, and maintenance, allowing you to focus on strategic aspects of your investments.

4. **Streamline Operations:** Implement systems and processes to streamline operations across your portfolio. This might include using property management software, creating standardized procedures for maintenance and rent collection, and developing efficient communication channels with tenants and contractors.

Monitoring and Adjusting Your Strategy

Scaling your portfolio requires ongoing monitoring and adjustment:

1. **Track Performance:** Regularly review the performance of your properties, including rental income, expenses, and overall return on investment. Use financial reports and performance metrics to identify areas for improvement and ensure your portfolio is meeting your goals.
2. **Adjust Your Strategy:** Be prepared to adjust your strategy based on market conditions and performance data. This might involve selling underperforming properties, exploring new investment opportunities, or revising your financial goals.
3. **Stay Informed:** Keep up-to-date with changes in the real estate market, financing options, and regulatory requirements. Staying informed will help you make informed decisions and adapt to evolving market conditions.

Conclusion

Scaling your real estate portfolio offers the potential for increased income, diversification, and long-term wealth building. By carefully planning your expansion, finding and evaluating new properties, and managing your portfolio effectively, you can achieve successful growth and maximize the benefits of your real estate investments. Remember, strategic growth and continuous learning are key to navigating the journey from a single property investor to a successful real estate portfolio owner.

Chapter 10: Navigating Market Changes and Future Trends

Congratulations on building and scaling your real estate portfolio! As you continue to grow and thrive in the real estate investment world, it's crucial to stay informed about market changes and emerging trends. The real estate market is dynamic, influenced by economic factors, technological advancements, and evolving consumer preferences. In this final chapter, we'll explore how to navigate market changes and leverage future trends to ensure your investments remain successful.

Understanding Market Cycles

Real estate markets go through cycles, influenced by broader economic conditions. Understanding these cycles can help you make informed decisions and optimize your investment strategy:

1.   **Expansion:** During an expansion phase, economic growth is strong, leading to increased demand for real estate. Property values and rents typically rise, providing opportunities for higher returns. Look for signs of expansion, such as job growth, rising consumer confidence, and increasing property values.

2.   **Peak:** At the peak of the market cycle, demand is high, and prices are at their highest. While this can be a profitable time to sell, be cautious about overpaying for new investments. Consider diversifying your portfolio or focusing on properties with stable demand.

3.   **Contraction:** In a contraction phase, economic growth slows, and property values may decline. Rental demand can weaken, leading to lower rental income. During this phase, focus on maintaining your existing properties, managing expenses, and being selective with new investments.

4.   **Recovery:** The recovery phase follows a contraction, with the market gradually improving.

Property values and rental demand start to rise again. This can be an opportune time to acquire new properties at lower prices and prepare for the next expansion phase.

Embracing Technological Advances

Technology is transforming the real estate industry, offering new tools and opportunities for investors. Here's how to leverage technology to enhance your investment strategy:

1. **Property Management Software:** Invest in property management software to streamline operations. These platforms can handle tasks such as rent collection, maintenance requests, and tenant communication, improving efficiency and organization.
2. **Data Analytics:** Use data analytics to gain insights into market trends, property performance, and investment opportunities. Analyzing data can help you make informed decisions, identify emerging markets, and optimize your portfolio.
3. **Virtual Tours and Listings:** Embrace virtual tours and online listings to reach a broader audience. Virtual tours allow potential tenants or buyers to

view properties remotely, increasing visibility and attracting interest from out-of-town prospects.

4.   **Smart Home Technology**: Consider integrating smart home technology into your properties. Features like smart thermostats, security systems, and energy-efficient appliances can enhance tenant satisfaction and make your properties more attractive in a competitive market.

Adapting to Changing Consumer Preferences

Consumer preferences in real estate are evolving, influenced by lifestyle changes and societal trends. Stay ahead of these trends to ensure your properties remain desirable:

1.   **Sustainable and Green Living**: Many tenants and buyers are prioritizing sustainability and energy efficiency. Consider investing in green upgrades, such as solar panels, energy-efficient windows, and sustainable materials, to attract environmentally-conscious renters and buyers.

2.   **Flexible Living Spaces**: The rise of remote work has increased demand for flexible living spaces. Properties with home office options, extra bedrooms, and adaptable layouts are becoming more appealing.

Ensure your properties can accommodate these evolving needs.

3. **Community Amenities**: Invest in properties located in neighborhoods with desirable amenities, such as parks, dining options, and recreational facilities. A strong sense of community and access to amenities can enhance property value and attract tenants.

4. **Health and Wellness**: Health and wellness trends are influencing real estate preferences. Features like clean air systems, wellness rooms, and access to outdoor spaces are becoming more sought after. Consider incorporating these elements into your property upgrades.

Preparing for Economic Uncertainty

Economic uncertainty can impact real estate markets, so it's essential to be prepared:

1. **Diversification**: Diversify your portfolio across different property types and geographic locations to reduce risk. Diversification can help mitigate the impact of market fluctuations and economic downturns.

2. **Emergency Fund**: Maintain an emergency fund to cover unexpected expenses or periods of

reduced rental income. Having financial reserves can provide stability during economic challenges and ensure you can manage your properties effectively.

3. **Market Research:** Continuously monitor market conditions and stay informed about economic indicators. Regularly review market trends, interest rates, and local developments to anticipate potential impacts on your investments.

Navigating market changes and leveraging future trends are key to maintaining a successful real estate portfolio. By understanding market cycles, embracing technology, adapting to consumer preferences, and preparing for economic uncertainty, you can ensure that your investments remain robust and profitable. Stay proactive, informed, and flexible to thrive in the ever-evolving world of real estate investing. With these strategies, you'll be well-equipped to continue your journey and achieve long-term success in the dynamic real estate market.

Conclusion: Embracing Financial Freedom and Building Wealth

Congratulations on reaching the final chapter of this guide! Your journey into real estate has not only opened the door to potential investments but has also paved the way for a broader understanding of financial literacy and freedom. As you move forward, remember that the principles of financial success go beyond just buying and managing properties—they encompass the broader goals of financial independence and wealth-building.

The path to financial freedom is akin to creating a masterpiece; it requires thoughtful planning, consistent effort, and a clear vision. At the heart of this journey is a commitment to learning and applying financial principles that set the foundation for lasting success. By now, you've grasped the importance of understanding financial concepts, whether it's budgeting, saving, investing, or managing debt. Each of these elements plays a critical role in achieving the ultimate goal of financial independence.

Building wealth isn't just about accumulating assets; it's about making informed decisions that align with your long-term financial goals. As you continue on this path, remember that each step you take toward enhancing your financial literacy is a step closer to realizing your dreams of financial freedom. Embrace the knowledge you've gained and apply it thoughtfully to make choices that support your vision of a secure and prosperous future.

Financial freedom allows you to live life on your terms. It's about having the flexibility to pursue your passions, enjoy the fruits of your labor, and make decisions without being constrained by financial limitations. Achieving this freedom involves a combination of strategic planning, disciplined saving, and smart investing. Keep your focus on long-term goals, and don't be swayed by short-term temptations or setbacks.

Building a legacy of wealth is more than just personal gain; it's about creating opportunities and security for future generations. Whether it's through wise investments, saving strategies, or simply teaching financial principles to those you care about, the impact of your financial decisions can extend beyond your own life and contribute to the well-being of your family and community.

As you embark on this journey, stay curious and open to new learning experiences. The world of finance is ever-evolving, and keeping up with changes and trends will help you stay ahead. Invest in yourself by continuously enhancing your financial knowledge and adapting your strategies as needed.

So, here's to your continued success in achieving financial freedom and building lasting wealth. With the insights you've gained and the commitment to applying them, you're well-equipped to navigate the path ahead. Remember, financial freedom isn't just a destination; it's a way of life. Embrace the journey with confidence, and may your financial future be as bright and rewarding as you envision.

Cheers to a future filled with financial independence, prosperity, and the freedom to live life to the fullest!